MW00893387

It was a cold January day and I was alone in my cell at the Los Angeles County Animal Shelter.

I was very sad. My owner had taken me here and just left me. He told the shelter that I was "too much work" and had "too much energy." I didn't understand! This was how God created me.

I prayed that someone would save me. I didn't like it here...it was lonely and scary.

A few days later a woman came to the shelter. She was kind and said hello to all the dogs but came specifically to my cell and smiled at me.

My heart leapt, and I could feel it in my bones. "She's going to rescue me!" I thought to myself.

And...I was right!

The surprises didn't stop there. She took me to my new home and I got to meet my dad!

And wait...

...brothers, too?!

I was in heaven.

I'd never felt so safe or loved.

But in the back of my mind for a while, I couldn't help but feel a little worried that my new mom and dad might return me to the shelter like my first owner had. Would they think I was "too much work" and had "too much energy" like he did?

Something in my heart told me that they were different. They treated me like part of the family. They told me over and over, "Hurley, we love you! We'll never let you go."

I started to notice when we went out for walks that some people seemed to be mad at us and give us mean looks. Some of them were even afraid of me.

"Keep your pit bull away from me!" a man once shouted at my mom.

I didn't understand. I loved everyone! I just wanted to kiss and play with whoever I met.

After the best two years of my life, my mom's best friend came over to our house with a surprise: a puppy! I could tell my mom and dad adored this little one.

After a while, my mom's friend left, and the puppy stayed! Oh no – were they replacing me?

They weren't. They were giving me a sister. They named her Wednesday. I found out that her owner had also given her up.

I think she was too young to understand.

She was lucky.

At the beginning, I felt jealous of Wednesday because I could see how much my family loved her. But I couldn't help but love her, too.

We became best friends.

I decided that I would protect her and never let anyone hurt her.

Time went on and Wednesday got bigger...

...but she didn't seem to notice.

We love to play together!

Wednesday likes to nap with Dad.

I like to take selfies with Mom.

I let Wednesday think she's in charge.

Because I love her so, so much.

Sometimes we get in trouble, but Mom and Dad always forgive us.

"It's because we're so cute," Wednesday says.

One day Wednesday and I got out of our backyard and ran across the street to the park. We saw a couple of other dogs and ran up to play. They didn't like that, and they started to attack Wednesday! I wouldn't let them. I stood in front of her and fought them off!

I got badly hurt, but I saved her life.

The other dogs' owners yelled at my mom and called Wednesday and me "mean pit bulls." I didn't understand! Why was it my fault? I was only protecting the most important puppy in the world.

Mom and Dad stood up for Wednesday and me,
like they always do when people say things that
aren't true. I knew they'd never stop loving us.

In a few weeks, I healed and got stronger.

Soon enough, Wednesday and I were back playing together again.

Something important that I've learned in my life is that not everyone will love you for who you are.

That's ok.

Be who you are anyway, and the right ones will come into your life and never leave.

Hurley in his cell at the animal shelter

Hurley and Mom about to go on the freedom drive
home!

Hurley and Dad

Hurley in his new backyard

Hurley and his new friend Gunnar

Hurley and Mom taking selfies

Kitty brothers, Jack and Hopkins

New sister Wednesday arrives

Hurley getting used to his new role as big brother

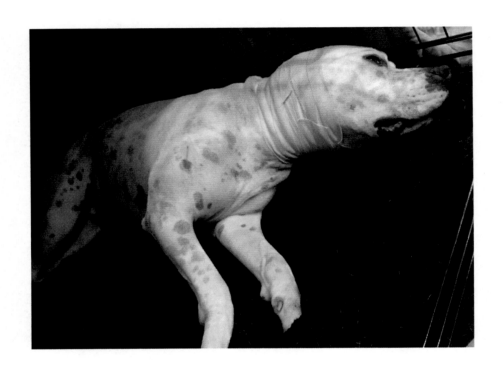

Hurley after saving Wednesday's life!

Playing again after he healed up

Mom, Dad, Wednesday and Hurley

ABOUT THE AUTHOR

Di is an actress and writer who lives in Southern California with her husband, stepchildren and menagerie of pets. If you share her love of pit bulls and kitties, follow her on social media for nonstop laughs and entertainment.
@aTaleOfPitties

69652725R00024

Made in the USA
Middletown, DE
21 September 2019